HOW CODING WORKS

by George Anthony Kulz

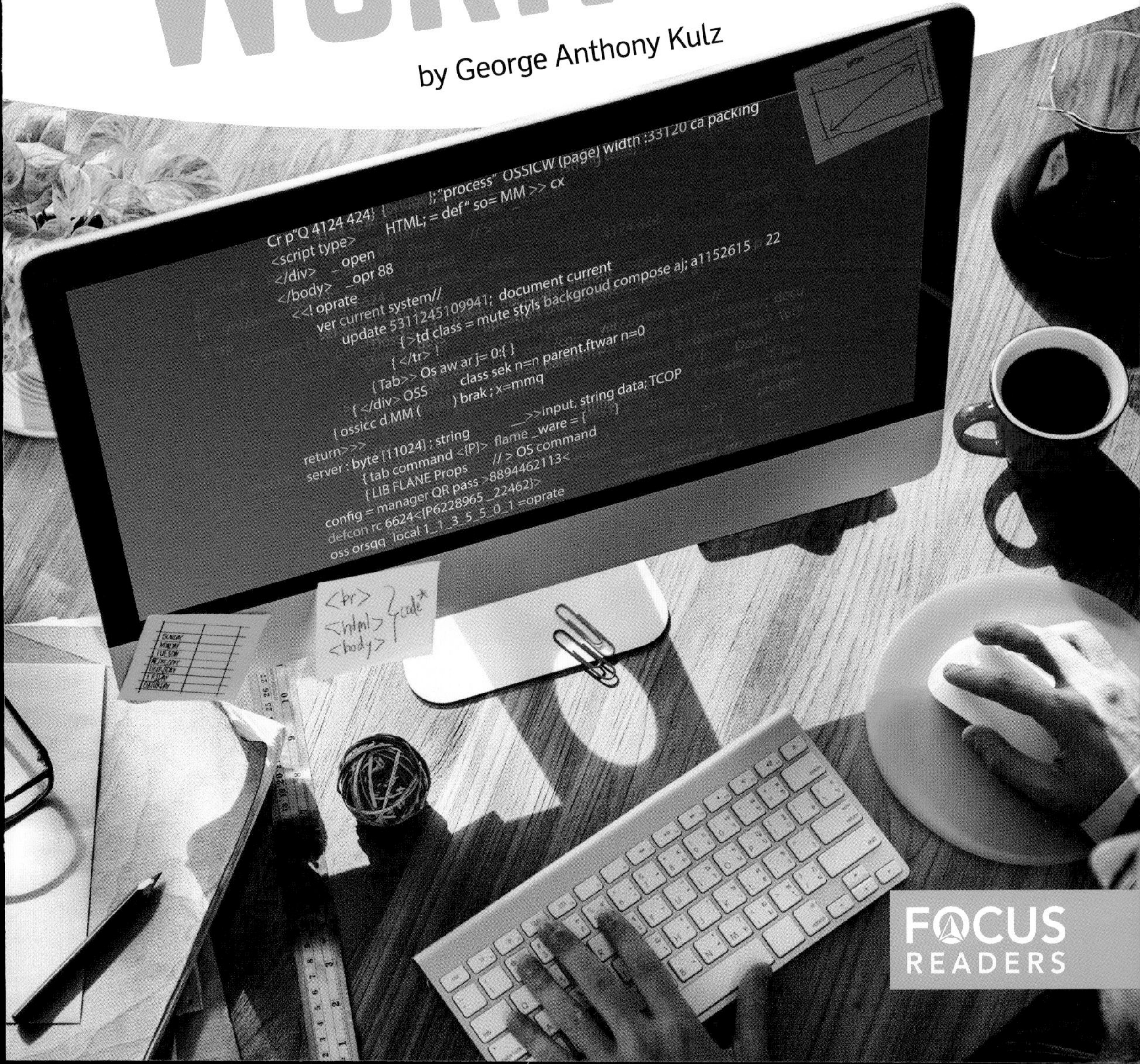

FOCUS READERS

WWW.FOCUSREADERS.COM

Focus Readers is distributed by North Star Editions:
sales@northstareditions.com | 888-417-0195

Produced for Focus Readers by Red Line Editorial.

Content Consultant: Dr. Sherali Zeadally, Associate Professor, College of Communication and Information, University of Kentucky

Photographs ©: Rawpixel.com/Shutterstock Images, cover, 1; PunkbarbyO/Shutterstock Images, 4–5; Gorodenkoff/Shutterstock Images, 7; JTaI/Shutterstock Images, 8–9; Red Line Editorial, 11; Dragon Images/Shutterstock Images, 12–13; iinspiration/Shutterstock Images, 15; hanss/Shutterstock Images, 16; Phil's Mommy/Shutterstock Images, 19; REDPIXEL.PL/Shutterstock Images, 20–21; Chat Karen Studio/Shutterstock Images, 23; Mr. Kosal/Shutterstock Images, 24–25; omihay/Shutterstock Images, 27; antoniodiaz/Shutterstock Images, 28

Library of Congress Cataloging-in-Publication Data
Library of Congress Cataloging-in-Publication Data is available on the Library of Congress website.

ISBN
978-1-64185-328-6 (hardcover)
978-1-64185-386-6 (paperback)
978-1-64185-502-0 (ebook pdf)
978-1-64185-444-3 (hosted ebook)

Printed in the United States of America
Mankato, MN
October, 2018

ABOUT THE AUTHOR

George Anthony Kulz holds a master's degree in computer engineering. He is a member of the Society of Children's Book Writers and Illustrators and has taken courses at the Institute of Children's Literature and the Gotham Writers' Workshop. He writes for children and adults.

TABLE OF CONTENTS

WHAT IS CODE?

A soccer player kicks the ball. It soars past the goalie and into the net. The crowd shouts and cheers. The player, off balance, falls onto the field. But no one is hurt. The soccer player isn't human. It's a robot. In fact, all the players are robots. They run, kick, and pass the ball.

Code controls a robot's actions. It tells this robot how to move its arms and legs.

The robots seem to do these things without anyone controlling them. Yet all robots are controlled by something. Each robot has a small computer inside it. The computer is like a brain for the robot. A brain controls a person's body. In a robot, the computer tells the robot's body what to do.

Unlike a person's brain, a robot's computer cannot think for itself. It must be told what to do. That is what code is for. Code is a set of instructions that tells a computer what to do. It can be used for simple actions, such as moving forward. It can also be used for complicated actions, such as passing a soccer ball.

The computer inside a robot is also called the controller.

Code breaks each action down into simple steps. It tells the computer what to do for each step. The computer follows the steps to complete the action. Together, all these steps make up the robot's **program**.

STEPS TO SOLVE A PROBLEM

Many steps go into making a program. First, the programmer creates an algorithm. An algorithm is a list of steps to solve a problem. For example, a robot vacuum's problem is that the floor is dirty. The algorithm tells the robot how to clean the floor. It breaks this task down into simple steps.

Code helps a robot vacuum cleaner map a room and avoid hitting furniture.

First, the robot must start in one corner of the room. It must move straight across the room. Next, the robot must move forward to a new part of the carpet. Then the robot must travel back across the room. The robot must repeat these steps until it has cleaned the whole room. And it must not bump into anything as it moves.

An algorithm includes all these steps. Some steps are done in order. The robot must move across the room one way before it goes back the other way. Other steps are done at the same time. As the robot moves, it must also watch for things in its way.

ROBOT MOVEMENT ALGORITHM

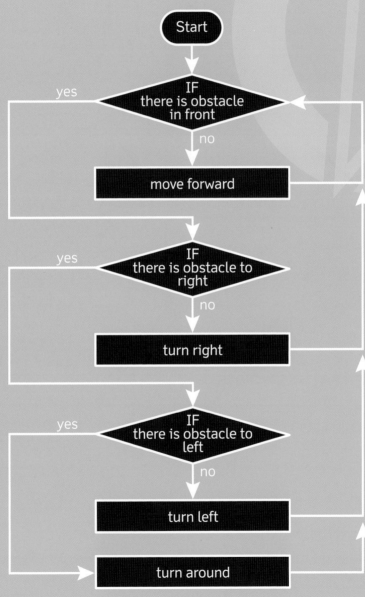

SPEAKING TO MACHINES

After creating an algorithm, coders choose a programming language. Programming languages are ways to write code. They help change the algorithm into instructions a computer can understand.

Computers can only understand machine language. This language uses zeroes and ones to form instructions.

Programmers must convert their algorithms into instructions a computer can follow.

However, instructions in this language tend to be very long. And it is the hardest language for people to understand. For these reasons, programmers often write code using a different programming language. This code will be translated to machine language later on.

WHY MACHINE LANGUAGE?

Machine language is written with zeroes and ones. These numbers turn parts of the computer on or off. A zero means off, and a one means on. When a computer part is on, electricity flows through it. This is how information moves in a computer. Every computer has its own machine language. Machine language code for one computer won't work on another one.

```
    <link rel="stylesheet" href="http://loca...
    <script type="text/javascript" src="http://localhost/javas...
  <script type="text/javascript">
    (function(){
      onLoaded: function(request) {
        if (request.name == 'log_error') return;
        log.trace("Ajax.Request: " + (request.name || request.url.substr(0,
          )) + "...");
      },
      onComplete: function(request) {
        if (request.name == 'log_error') return;
      },
      onException: function(request, e) {
        if (request.name == 'log_error') return;
        ...(request.url ... ': ' + e.name + ' | ' + e.message + ' | '
```

The programming language Java is used to create parts of many websites.

Some languages, such as Java, use words to create instructions. Java is an object-oriented language. It uses sets of instructions called **classes**. Programmers use classes to create **objects**. Every object has properties, or things it knows. The object also has methods, or things it can do.

Many objects work together to help the program do its job. For instance, a program might show students' grades. An

OTHER LANGUAGES FOR CODING

HTML

Controls the appearance of the text, images, and links on web pages

CSS

Creates the layout and design elements of web pages

JAVASCRIPT

Adds interactive effects to web pages

PHP

Helps web browsers access web pages

SQL

Allows users to update, search, and modify data

object would know one student's grade. That object's methods would use the student's test scores to calculate the grade.

Other languages are used for a unique type of problem. They are known as domain-specific languages. One example is Structured Query Language (SQL). This language is only used with **databases**. SQL has instructions that put **data** into or get data out of a database.

Visual programming languages use pictures instead of words. One example is Scratch. Coders connect colored blocks to create instructions. Together, the blocks create the steps of a program.

CREATING INSTRUCTIONS

All programming languages have the same three parts. They are syntax, semantics, and pragmatics. Syntax tells what instructions will be used in the language. For example, a language called Scratch uses colored blocks with words in them. Each block is an instruction. The entire set of blocks makes up this language's syntax. Coders can put the blocks together in many ways.

Semantics explains the meaning of all the instructions in the language. In Scratch, one orange block says "when right arrow key pressed." A blue block says "move 10 steps." When these blocks are joined together, the character on the screen will move 10 steps when the player presses the right arrow key.

In Scratch, blocks are different colors depending on what kind of instructions they give.

Pragmatics tells what happens inside the computer when instructions are used. This is when the code is translated to machine language. That way, the computer knows how to respond to the instructions.

EVENTS, CONDITIONS, AND LOOPS

Programmers translate each step in the algorithm into code. They use instructions from their chosen language. There are hundreds of programming languages in the world today. New ones are still being created. Each has its own set of instructions. Common instructions involve events, conditions, and loops.

Coders write step-by-step instructions for a computer to follow.

An event is an action that a computer recognizes. Pressing an arrow key is an event. So is saying a word into a microphone. The program responds to the event with a specific action. For example, pressing the space bar might make a game character jump.

A condition is a true-or-false statement that determines what the program does next. If a condition is true, one set of steps will be **executed**. Otherwise, a different set of steps will be executed. A condition can depend on an event or on data. For instance, a number might get larger when clicked on. Or it might turn red if it is less than zero.

Clicking the mouse is one event a computer might recognize.

A loop tells the computer to repeat a set of steps. Some loops repeat steps a certain number of times. Other loops repeat steps until an event happens or a condition is true. For example, a game character may walk forward until a player presses a button. Then the character will turn and walk the other way.

CHAPTER 5

TRANSLATING IT BACK

After all the code is written, the program is almost ready to use. But first, the code must be translated from the programming language into machine language.

Programs can be translated by a **compiler** or by an **interpreter**. A compiler translates all the lines of code at once.

One program may contain thousands or even millions of lines of code.

When the compiler is done translating, it creates an executable. An executable is a program or file that a computer can understand and use to perform a specific task. The executable can be used by anyone who wants to use the program. Users can run the program anytime after it is compiled.

An interpreter looks at one line of code at a time. It translates that line and runs it. Then the interpreter goes to the next line. There is no executable. The program must be interpreted every time it is run.

Some languages need both a compiler and an interpreter. One example of this is Java. This language is first compiled

An operating system, such as Windows 10, is an example of an executable.

into bytecode. Bytecode is similar to an executable. But when a user runs the bytecode, it is interpreted and run one line at a time.

Interpreted languages get translated very quickly into machine language.

One program can be used many times. Some programs can even be used on different devices.

But the program takes longer to run. In contrast, compilers often take a long time to change programming languages into machine language. But the program runs quickly once it has been compiled.

Once a program has been compiled or interpreted, it is ready to use. Anyone can use the program. Users do not need to read or write code. Instead, the program responds to their actions. Its step-by-step instructions help the device do its job.

LINES OF CODE

A line of code is a single step in a program. The simplest programs have only one line of code. One example is a program that displays the words "Hello, World!" One of the largest programs controls Google's website. This program has two billion lines of code.

FOCUS ON
HOW CODING WORKS

Write your answers on a separate piece of paper.

1. Write a paragraph explaining the steps that go into making a program.

2. If you were creating a program, what programming language would you use? Why?

3. Which language is made specifically for databases?
    - **A.** SQL
    - **B.** Scratch
    - **C.** machine language

4. What might happen if a programmer wrote code for only some of the steps of an algorithm?
    - **A.** The computer would do the steps faster.
    - **B.** The computer would do the steps backwards.
    - **C.** The computer would not be able to do all the steps.

Answer key on page 32.

GLOSSARY

classes
Sets of instructions that are used to create a particular type of object in a computer program.

compiler
A program that turns all the code in a program into machine language at one time.

data
Information collected to study or track something.

databases
Systems that use computers to store and organize large amounts of information.

executed
Done according to a plan.

interpreter
A program that turns code into machine language one line at a time.

objects
Sets of ideas and actions used to form one piece of a computer program.

program
A set of instructions that are given to a machine so it can perform an action.

TO LEARN MORE

BOOKS

Smibert, Angie. *All About Coding*. Lake Elmo, MN: Focus Readers, 2017.

Wainewright, Max. *How to Code: A Step-by-Step Guide to Computer Coding*. New York: Sterling Children's Books, 2016.

Woodcock, Jon. *Coding Projects in Scratch*. New York: DK Publishing, 2016.

NOTE TO EDUCATORS

Visit **www.focusreaders.com** to find lesson plans, activities, links, and other resources related to this title.

INDEX

Answer Key: 1. Answers will vary; **2.** Answers will vary; **3.** A; **4.** C